LOOKING BACK

# JAPAN UNDER THE SHOGUNS

## 1185–1868

**LOOKING BACK**

# JAPAN UNDER THE SHOGUNS

## 1185–1868

MAVIS PILBEAM

RAINTREE
STECK-VAUGHN
PUBLISHERS
A Steck-Vaughn Company

*Austin, Texas*

*To my dear friend, Leslie*



Editors: Nicola Barber, Pamela Wells
Designer: Traffika Publishing Limited
Picture research: Victoria Brooker
Maps: Nick Hawken
Production: Jenny Mulvanny

Consultant: Dr. Gordon Daniels, Reader in Japanese History, Department of History, University of Sheffield

**Library of Congress Cataloging-in-Publication Data**

Pilbeam, Mavis.
Japan under the shoguns, 1185–1868 / Mavis Pilbeam.
p. cm. — (Looking back)
Includes bibliographical references and index.
Summary: Discusses the history of Japan during the nearly 700 years when the country was under the rule of military warlords, or shoguns.
ISBN 0-8172-5431-5
1. Japan — History — 1185–1868 — Juvenile literature. [1. Japan — History — 1185–1868.] I. Title. II. Series.
DS835.P55 1999
452'.02 — dc21 98-26515
CIP AC

Printed in Spain
Bound in the United States
1 2 3 4 5 6 7 8 9 0 LB 02 01 00 99 98

## Acknowledgments

**Cover** (main image) Adina Tovy/Robert Harding Picture Library (background image) Private Collection/Bridgeman Art Library **page 7** Getty Images **page 8** Werner Forman **page 10** Trustees of the British Museum **page 11** Werner Forman **page 12** Trustees of the British Museum **page 13** Trustees of the British Museum **page 15** (top) John Greenlees (bottom) Trustees of the British Museum **page 17** Museum of the Imperial Collections, Sannomaru Shozokan, Tokyo **page 19** Trustees of the British Museum **page 21** Adina Tovy/Robert Harding Picture Library **page 22** Werner Forman **page 23** Trustees of the British Museum **page 25** (top) Werner Forman (bottom) Werner Forman **page 26** Nigel Blythe Photography/Robert Harding Picture Library **page 27** Trustees of the British Museum **page 29** Trustees of the British Museum **page 30** Werner Forman **page 31** Trustees of the British Museum **page 32** Werner Forman **page 34** © Gregory Irvine **page 35** Trustees of the British Museum **page 36** Museum of the Imperial Collections, Sannomaru Shozokan, Tokyo **page 37** Robert Harding Picture Library **page 38** Percival David Foundation, London/Bridgeman Art Library **page 41** Courtesy of the Trustees of the V&A **page 42** Trustees of the British Museum **page 43** Trustees of the British Museum **page 44** Trustees of the British Museum **page 46** Courtesy of the Trustees of the V&A **page 47** Nigel Blythe/Robert Harding Picture Library **page 49** Trustees of the British Museum **page 50** Gift of W. G Russell Allen, Courtesy, Museum of Fine Arts, Boston **page 51** Copyright Gregory Irvine **page 52** Trustees of the British Museum **page 53** Idemitsu Museum of Arts, Tokyo **page 54** (top and bottom) Trustees of the British Museum **page 55** Werner Forman **page 56** Trustees of the British Museum **page 57** Trustees of the British Museum **page 59** Adina Tovy/Robert Harding Picture Library

# CONTENTS

# INTRODUCTION

This book tells the story of nearly 700 years of Japanese history, from 1185 to 1868. During this time Japan was ruled almost continuously by military warlords called shoguns. The Japanese emperors remained in the capital, Kyoto, as religious and cultural leaders throughout this period. The Japanese people believed that their emperors were gods who were directly descended from the Sun Goddess. Therefore, the shoguns always treated the imperial family with respect. The emperors continued to reign, carrying out religious ceremonies and safeguarding Japan's ancient traditions. However, it was the shoguns who ruled the country, trying to ensure both peace and prosperity for the Japanese people.

The first shogun, Minamoto Yoritomo, received his title in 1192, but his rule really began in 1185 when he defeated his rivals and took control of the country. The military governments of the shoguns are known as shogunates: the first was the Kamakura Shogunate (1192–1333), the second was the Muromachi (1338–1573), and the third, the Tokugawa (1603–1867). The shogunate finally came to an end in 1868 when the rule of the emperor was restored.

**A CLOSER LOOK**

The shogun's full title was *seii taishōgun*, which means "Great Barbarian-Quelling Generalissimo." The very first shoguns were generals sent by the emperor to fight rebellious clans along Japan's northern frontiers in the 8th century. These early shoguns had no real power, but the title was brought back into use in 1192 for the military ruler, Minamoto Yoritomo.

## JAPAN

Japan is a string of islands in the Pacific Ocean to the east of the Asian mainland. Its nearest neighbors are Korea, China, and Russia. Geographical factors have affected Japan's history. First, as an island country 125 miles (200 km) from the nearest mainland,

*At 12,388 feet (3,776 m), Mount Fuji is the highest mountain in Japan. It is a dormant volcano and is regarded as sacred.*

Japan maintained its independence from foreign powers until the late 19th century. Secondly, within Japan, the landscape of steep mountains and deep, narrow valleys made communications difficult. This encouraged the development of tight-knit local communities that were hostile to the central government and that often attacked each other.

**A CLOSER LOOK**

Most Japanese names have four syllables arranged in two pairs:
Mi-na/mo-to Yo-ri/to-mo
Each syllable ends in a vowel (a, e, i, o, u). Sometimes a syllable is just a vowel on its own:
To-ku/ga-wa I-e/ya-su
(Note that surnames always come first in Japanese)

Pronunciation: the consonants (m, t, y, etc.) have almost the same sounds as English. The vowels are:
a which sounds more like the u in English "hut"
e sounds like e in "bet"
i sounds like ee in "feet"
o sounds like o in "hot"
ō sounds like o in "or"
u is like u in "put"
ū sounds like oo in "boot"

## HOW DO WE KNOW?

Our knowledge of the shoguns comes from a wide variety of sources. There are many buildings and everyday articles from shogun times still in existence. Scholars study old documents relating to government and trade, such as Yoritomo's first instructions to his officials. Some early foreign visitors to Japan wrote detailed diaries describing what they saw. Plays and illustrated books tell us much about everyday life. Works of art, especially prints and paintings, depict all kinds of people at work and play, and help us to understand the changing tastes of the times. Finally, many people in modern Japan continue to practice martial arts and the tea ceremony as they did in the past, providing a connection through to the present day.

# JAPAN BEFORE THE SHOGUNS

*Rows of pottery figures, called* haniwa, *were placed around the tombs of Kofun leaders (see page 9) as guardians. This helmeted* haniwa *warrior is fully armed for battle.*

Japanese history and civilization stretch back into the distant past. Archaeologists have found stone implements and some animal and human bones which suggest that people lived in Japan from 30,000 B.C., or even earlier.

From about 10,000 B.C. Japanese prehistory is divided into three periods: Jōmon, Yayoi and Kofun. Jōmon means "cord-marked," and the Jōmon Period (10,000–300 B.C.) is named after a kind of pottery decorated with patterns made by pressing cords into the wet clay. This was probably the first pottery to be made anywhere in the world. People of the Jōmon Period lived peacefully in pit-dwellings. They ate wild plants and caught fish and whales from dugout canoes. Shellfish were particularly popular, and huge dumps of empty shells indicate to archaeologists the position and age of settlements.

The Yayoi Period (300 B.C.–A.D. 300) is named after a place called Yayoi in Tokyo where a different kind of pottery was first dug up by archaeologists. During this period many newcomers arrived from the Asian mainland and intermarried peacefully with the Jōmon peoples. They brought with them metalworking techniques in bronze and iron. They also introduced rice growing, which has continued right through to modern times.

Settled communities grew up, but disputes over land began to break out between neighboring tribes.

At the beginning of the Kofun ("Old Tomb") Period (A.D. 300–710), a power struggle developed among over 100 small kingdoms, each with its own leader. The status of these leaders is shown by their elaborate graves that were covered by massive earth mounds, from which the period takes its name. There were several centers of power, particularly Yamato in the west of Honshū (the main island), and Izumo on the Japan Sea coast, but eventually the leaders of Yamato overcame all opposition. They established themselves as emperors and claimed descent from Amaterasu, the Sun Goddess.

## EARLY RECORDS

The *Kojiki* (Records of Ancient Matters) and the *Nihonshoki* (Chronicles of Japan) were written by the new leaders of Japan to strengthen their claims to the throne. They were the first records in the Japanese language. They contain some historical fact, but mostly they relate the myths that had been passed down by word of mouth over many centuries. They tell of the creation of the Japanese islands. They also relate how the Sun Goddess, Amaterasu, founded the imperial family after quarreling with her brother, Susa-no-o. This story was a way of describing the power struggle between the provinces of Yamato (represented by Amaterasu) and Izumo (Susa-no-o).

### A CLOSER LOOK

**From the 5th century there was a growing exchange of gifts between Japanese leaders and the Chinese court. During the 7th and 8th centuries, even more exotic goods reached Japan from as far away as Persia along the Silk Road, a trade route that wound its way through the mountains and deserts of Central Asia. Emperor Shōmu collected many Silk Road treasures that, after his death in 749, his widow placed in the Shōsōin storehouse in Nara. During subsequent centuries, emperors would sometimes invite the shoguns to view these treasures. They are still in the Shōsōin storehouse after more than 1,000 years.**

## OUTSIDE INFLUENCES

The earliest mention of Japan is in Chinese records written between the 1st and the 3rd centuries A.D. Relations between Japan, China,

**A CLOSER LOOK**
The Japanese writing system uses thousands of ideographs borrowed from Chinese. Reading downward this says "shōgun."

and Korea grew in importance during the 5th century. At first, most new ideas reached Japan from Korea, which had close links with China. Large numbers of Koreans arrived in Japan, bringing new methods of textile production, metalwork, and pottery, in addition to ideas about architecture, town-planning, and government.

The two most important arrivals in Japan in about the mid-6th century were the Chinese writing system and Buddhism. Before this time, the Japanese had no method of writing, but the Chinese system allowed them to record laws, religious teaching, and historical accounts.

Buddhism was supported by Prince Shōtoku Taishi (574–622), one of the most important figures of this period. He built many temples, including Hōryūji Temple, the oldest surviving wooden building in the world. Shōtoku made governmental reforms based on Chinese ideas that emphasized

**A CLOSER LOOK**
Japanese written with Chinese ideographs (*kanji*) was used only by men. It was stiff and formal, with many Chinese words and expressions. However, during the Heian Period (A.D. 794–1185) a much simpler script developed, called *kana*. This script was more suitable for writing pure Japanese. It was used by both men and women to express their feelings in poetry and prose. In the 11th century, Lady Murasaki wrote the world's first novel, *The Tale of Genji*, which tells of the life and loves of Genji, the "Shining Prince."

*A shell game box (see page 49) painted with a scene from* The Tale of Genji. *Prince Genji (bottom left) gazes at some beautiful ladies from the Heian court with their many-layered robes and long hair.*

harmony. He started direct contacts with the Chinese court that lasted until 894.

New capital cities were also constructed on Chinese models. Nara, built in 710, was based on a grid pattern of roads running north-south and east-west. The Nara Period lasted from 710 until 794. During this time the whole land was under imperial control, and the central government collected taxes of rice, fish, salt, seaweed, and essential goods, such as pottery, from the provinces for use in the capital.

## RELIGION IN JAPAN

*Musicians perform* gagaku, *the ancient court music of Japan, at the great Shintō shrine at Ise.*

Shintō, Japan's oldest religion, is practiced only in Japan. Shintō means "The Way of the Gods." People believed that guardian gods were present everywhere, in mountains, trees, and rice fields, in addition to the hearth and home. They thought that human beings were a part of the natural world and should live happily in harmony with nature, with the spirits of their ancestors, and with their neighbors. The chief deity was Amaterasu, the Sun Goddess, founder of the imperial family. Therefore, as her successors, emperors and empresses were also gods, responsible for leading religious ceremonies for the good of the people.

Japan's other main religion is Buddhism, which came from India via China and Korea in the 6th century. Buddhism was founded over 2,000 years ago by the Indian prince, Gautama. One day, he saw a dying man, and he decided to give up his luxurious life in order to find the cause of suffering and the truth about life. He eventually became the first Buddha, which means "one who understands the truth." Buddhism teaches that there are many paths to truth, and everyone can find salvation by giving up worldly desires and disciplining the mind without thoughts of self. Although Shintō and Buddhism are very different, both became equally important in Japan. Buddhist temples were often built next to

Shintō shrines. Buddhist monks also organized hospitals and schools.

Confucianism is named after the great Chinese thinker, Confucius (551–479 B.C.). It also came from China to Japan during the 6th century A.D. It was not a religion, but rather a set of ideas about how to control people's lives. Confucianism stated that a stable and happy society was based on everyone keeping to their proper place in life, showing respect to their elders and superiors. It was a major influence on Japanese society and government, especially under the Tokugawa Shogunate (1603–1867).

*The original Buddha (c. 563–483 B.C.) is called Shaka in Japanese Buddhism. During his search for the truth, Shaka spent six years with very little food or rest. His body turned black and almost wasted away, as shown in this small bronze sculpture.*

## THE HEIAN PERIOD

In 794, Emperor Kammu moved to a new capital, which he named Heiankyō, "city of peace and tranquillity." The Heian Period lasted for almost 400 years. From the late 9th century, Japan broke off its contacts with China, and a more Japanese way of life and culture began to develop in court circles. The arts of poetry and calligraphy achieved the highest perfection and Heiankyō, or Kyoto as it came to be called, is still regarded by the Japanese today as the cultural heart of Japan. Yet less than one percent of the population enjoyed this way of life—the emperor, the aristocrats, who held the top five ranks at court, and a few thousand officials and ladies-in-waiting. At the same time, large areas of Kyoto were inhabited by poor people who lived crowded together in tiny houses that were frequently flooded when the river burst its banks.

The tranquillity of court life was constantly disturbed by power struggles. The ambitious

Fujiwara family came to dominate the throne by acting as regents to inexperienced young emperors, virtually ruling on their behalf. They also arranged marriages between their daughters and emperors. Michinaga, the most powerful of all the Fujiwara, had four daughters married to imperial husbands and was grandfather to three emperors.

While these intrigues were going on in Kyoto, the central government gradually lost control of the provinces. In theory, all the land belonged to the emperor, but a number of warrior leaders took control of some land as private estates, and seized the taxes that should have gone to the emperor. These leaders also began to build up private armies, and this eventually led to a confrontation between the leading warrior clans, the Taira and the Minamoto. As a result, the peaceful Heian Period ended in the horror of the Gempei Wars (1180–1185).

## A CLOSER LOOK

The Taira family in the west and the Minamoto family in the east were the most powerful warrior families in 12th-century Japan. For a time the Taira gained supremacy over the Minamoto. They moved into Kyoto to try to dominate the court, just as the Fujiwara had done. However, when Emperor Go-Shirakawa turned against the Taira, the Minamoto leader, Yoritomo, saw his chance and declared war on the Taira in 1180. Yoritomo was not a great general and entrusted most of the campaigns to his brother, Yoshitsune (1159–1189). By 1183, the Taira had been driven from Kyoto. Yoshitsune then defeated them at Yashima and won a final, brilliant victory at the sea battle of Dannoura. The memory of the tragic rise and fall of the Taira survives in *The Tale of the Heike*, a narrative poem from the middle of the 13th century.

*The Battle of Yashima was fought at Yashima Island in the Inland Sea during March 1185.*

# The Kamakura Shogunate

The founder of the first warrior government was Minamoto Yoritomo (1147–1199), who made his headquarters at Kamakura in eastern Japan, about 250 miles (400 km) across the mountains from Kyoto. This marked the beginning of a new era. Instead of courtly aristocrats, Japan was now ruled by warriors who had their own customs and outlook. Yoritomo surrounded himself with loyal followers, from whom he demanded total devotion, and set about bringing security and justice to the whole country. In 1185 he obtained imperial permission to establish his supporters as supervisors of private estates around the country and military governors in the provinces.

*This map shows the four main islands of Japan and the location of places mentioned in the text.*

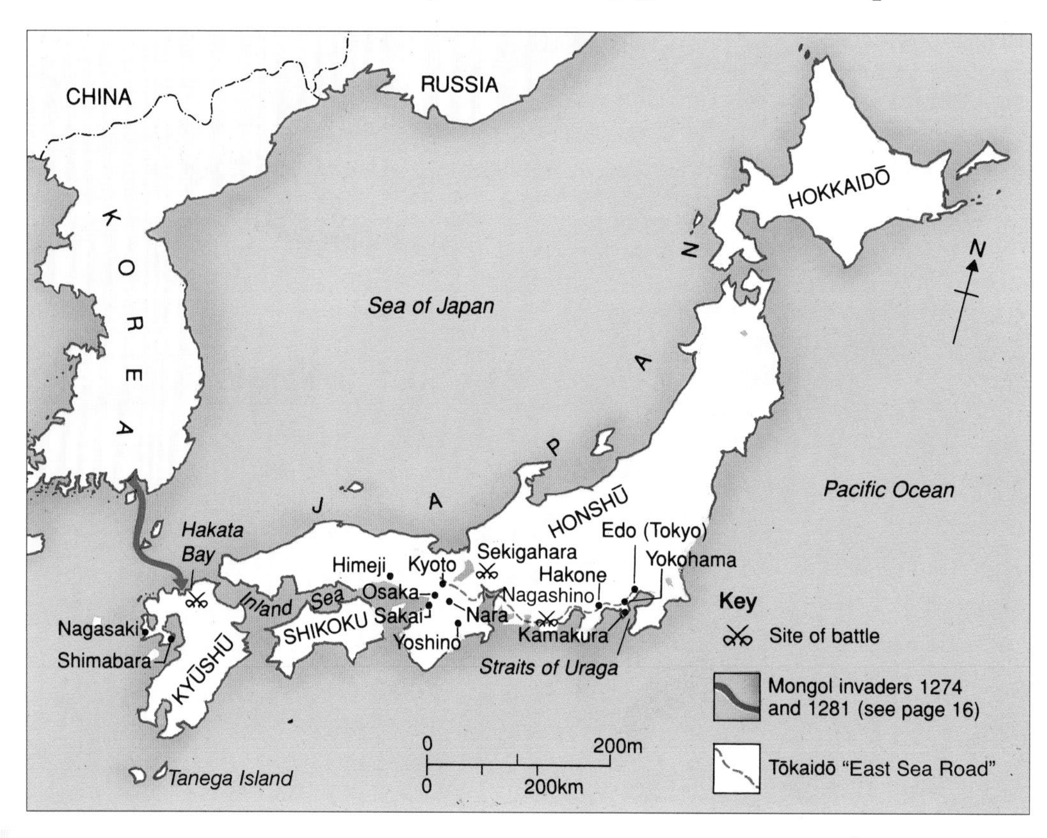

**A CLOSER LOOK**

Modern Kamakura (right) is a popular seaside town south of Tokyo. In the late 12th century, it was just a small fishing village, but because it was on the coast and backed by hills, it had excellent natural defenses. As a city, it was not as impressive as Kyoto. When the aristocratic Lady Nijō visited it in 1289, she wrote scathingly: "I found a spot that afforded a prospect of the city. How different from the view of Kyoto from the eastern hills! Houses hugged the mountain slope in terraced rows, huddled together like things stuffed in a pouch. I found it an altogether unattractive sight."

He also created new posts and government offices to deal with legal and financial matters. Although Kamakura was far from the emperor's court, Yoritomo maintained strong links with Kyoto because he still needed imperial approval to make his position safe. In 1192, the emperor finally recognized his authority by granting him the title of shogun.

*This portrait of Minamoto Yoritomo shows the "unifier and pacifier of Japan" in court dress.*

## MINAMOTO YORITOMO

At about the age of 13, Yoritomo took part in an unsuccessful military uprising in Kyoto. His father was killed, and he was captured by his enemies and exiled to eastern Japan. His captors treated him well and allowed him to practice his fighting skills. Eventually he married the daughter of one of his captors, a strong-willed woman called Hōjō Masako,

**A CLOSER LOOK**
Yoritomo's brother, Yoshitsune, became the most romantic figure in Japanese history after his violent death. Yoshitsune had a faithful servant called Benkei. Benkei was a warrior-monk who one day decided he would collect 1,000 weapons by challenging warriors crossing the Gōjō Bridge in Kyoto. With 999 weapons in his grasp, he thought he had an easy task when the slim figure of Yoshitsune approached. Much to his surprise Benkei found himself rolling, defeated, at the young hero's feet. Benkei was so impressed with Yoshitsune's valor that he begged to become his follower and accompanied him everywhere, even to death.

who later played a leading part in the shogunate's fortunes.

Although Yoritomo was one of the most influential figures in Japanese history, he is not as popular as his brother, Yoshitsune. This is because, out of suspicion and jealousy, Yorimoto treated Yoshitsune as his worst enemy, finally forcing him to commit suicide by *seppuku*, "cutting the stomach."

## THE HŌJŌ FAMILY

Yoritomo probably died in a riding accident. His two sons were weak, and they were both assassinated, leaving the shogunate in the hands of Yoritomo's wife and her family, the Hōjō, in 1219. The Hōjō did not become shoguns themselves, but gave the title to weak princes chosen from the Kyoto court and then ruled on their behalf as regents. The Hōjō remained in power for over a century. When the emperor tried to overthrow them in 1221, they withstood him and strengthened their authority over western Japan. They also survived two invasion attempts by the Mongols in 1274 and 1281. However, soon after this their power and popularity gradually declined. The crisis came when Emperor Go-Daigo launched a serious attack on the shogunate. Go-Daigo was victorious and brought the Kamakura Shogunate to an end in 1333.

## MONGOL INVASIONS

The most famous leader of the Mongols was a fierce warrior called Genghis Khan. He and his family conquered most of Asia, including China and Korea.

In the late 13th century his grandson, Kublai Khan, turned his attention to Japan. Calling himself

*The Japanese warrior Takezaki Suenaga, faces, a hail of arrows and a fireball aimed by a band of Mongol invaders. His curved sword and long bow contrast with the straight swords and shorter bows of his enemies. Takezaki presented these painted scrolls to the shogun as proof of his bravery and was richly rewarded.*

the "Lord of the Universe," he wrote threatening letters—all of which the Japanese leaders ignored. So, in 1274, Kublai attacked with a large force. At first, his troops landed successfully, but then his fleet was destroyed in a storm. Next, Kublai set up a Ministry for Conquering Japan. This time the Japanese beheaded all his messengers and built fortifications around Hakata Bay in Kyūshū. The Mongols returned in 1281, but again their ships were wrecked by a gale that the Japanese believed to be a *kamikaze*, "divine wind" sent by the gods to save them. However, although the country itself was safe, these invasions caused much hardship and discontent among many of the Japanese warriors. They had been forced to give service and resources for the war, but because no lands were won, the shogun had nothing to give them as a reward.

## KAMAKURA BUDDHISM

In the early Kamakura Period, many people were pessimistic, feeling that the peaceful days of the Heian Period were at an end. Even the monks had become worldly and warlike. Until this time,

Buddhism had been the religion mainly of the aristocracy. However, new sects of Buddhism began to develop that offered fresh hope to all.

A monk called Hōnen started the Pure Land sect, which taught that people could no longer be saved through their own efforts. However, Japanese Buddhists believed that there were many Buddhas. Hōnen said that one of these, named Amida, had promised all believers that they would be born into the Pure Land in the next life. All they had to do was to repeat his name, Amida, over and over again in perfect faith. One of Hōnen's disciples, Shinran, went to live among peasant farmers and gained many followers through his simple and lively roadside preaching.

In 1253, a Japanese monk called Nichiren created his own sect which taught that every individual, and the Japanese nation as a whole, could achieve perfection in this world. He even took the credit for the destruction of the Mongol fleets.

Zen, which came to Japan from China, was very different from the other new sects. Zen means "meditation," and Zen masters insisted that salvation could only be reached through each individual's effort of mind. Controlling the mind would lead to an understanding of life called "enlightenment." With its special way of life and arts, Zen gradually gained the support of the Kamakura Shogunate and wealthy merchants (see page 36).

## SOCIAL AND ECONOMIC CHANGE

In the Heian Period, the aristocracy regarded ordinary people as little more than animals whose job was to provide for the needs of the court. However, from the late 12th century, some farmers became more independent and began experimenting with improved farming methods, such as better irrigation and double-cropping. They probably sent a few goods to the markets that were developing in the Kyoto area. By the mid-13th century, Kamakura and other major cities all had busy markets. Thriving ports handled goods that had been collected as taxes to send to Kyoto. There was also considerable trade in luxury goods with China.

Traveling craftsworkers such as potters, weavers, and carpenters moved around the country selling their wares. In Kyoto, craftsworkers' guilds called *za* were set up. A *za* was a group of craftsworkers who paid a patron for protection from competitors and sold him goods that he could not get from his country estates. For the first time, a separate merchant class developed, made up of people who earned a living by buying and selling.

From early times, people in Japan paid for things with rice or cloth or by barter—the straight exchange of goods of equal value. However, copper coins imported from China gradually came into use. Moneylenders set up businesses, and many warriors borrowed from them and then got into debt. The government played little part in these changes, except for passing laws trying to stop people from becoming too rich. They forbade the use of coins and ordered the warriors to lead more frugal lives. But the tide could not be turned, and this commercial network continued to grow, changing the lives of people all over the country in the centuries to come.

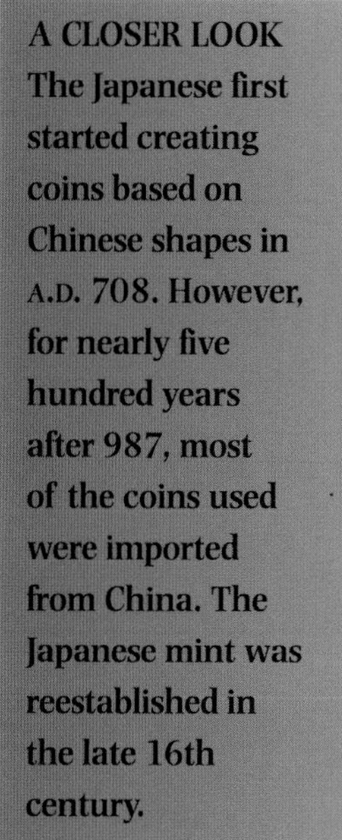

**A CLOSER LOOK**
**The Japanese first started creating coins based on Chinese shapes in A.D. 708. However, for nearly five hundred years after 987, most of the coins used were imported from China. The Japanese mint was reestablished in the late 16th century.**

*A silver coin struck at Edo in 1837*

*A silver coin of A.D. 708*

*A bronze coin of A.D. 760*

*A silver coin issued by Hideyoshi in 1587*

# Civil War and Reunification

The period after the defeat of the Kamakura Shogunate falls into two parts. First, under the Muromachi Shogunate (1338–1573) there was a gradual decline of central government leading to fierce civil war throughout the country. Then the shogunate was abolished temporarily, and Japan was reunified by three warriors who, one by one, led the country to peace. This time of reunification from about 1574–1600 is called the Momoyama Period. It marks the beginning of Japan's modern history.

## The Muromachi shoguns

Emperor Go-Daigo's chief ally in defeating the Kamakura Shogunate in 1333 was a Hōjō follower who had changed sides. His name was Ashikaga Takauji, (1305–1358). Takauji restored the emperor to power in Kyoto, but soon became dissatisfied with his policies. He imprisoned Go-Daigo and made the child-prince, Kōmyō, emperor in his place. After being imprisoned by Takauji, Emperor Go-Daigo escaped and set up his own court in Yoshino, 62 miles (100 km) to the south of Kyoto. For most of the 14th century Japan was in the strange position of having two emperors from different branches of the imperial line, one at the Southern Court of Yoshino, and the other at the Northern Court of Kyoto.

Takauji declared himself shogun in 1338 and based his headquarters in the Muromachi district of Kyoto. Unlike the Kamakura shoguns, the 15 Muromachi shoguns were all from the Ashikaga family, so this is often called the Ashikaga Shogunate. Takauji based his regime on the Kamakura model and, after an uncertain start, the shogunate quickly reached the height of its power in the late

**A CLOSER LOOK**

Of all the Ashikaga shoguns, the third, Yoshimitsu (1358–1408) is the most famous. He established control over the whole country and reunified the two imperial courts. Calling himself "King of Japan," he renewed contact with China and sent the Chinese emperor 3,000 swords. In return he received a gift of 30 million coins. Besides being a clever administrator and diplomat, Yoshimitsu was a man of culture. After handing over office to his son in 1395, he built a grand villa in Kyoto where he entertained artists and priests, created gardens, and held tea ceremonies, *Nō* theater performances, and poetry writing parties.

*The Temple of the Golden Pavilion is part of Yoshimitsu's villa in Kyoto.*

13th century, under the firm rule of Ashikaga Yoshimitsu. During the 14th century, however, disorder spread throughout the country. This was because the shoguns had failed to establish their authority in the eastern provinces, relying too much on the support and goodwill of their provincial officials. Many of these officials set themselves up as warlords and attacked each other in the Ōnin wars (1467–1477), during which the city of Kyoto was

**A CLOSER LOOK**

*Daimyō* were samurai leaders who became dominant in the late 14th century. Originally, they were officers of the shogun whose duties were to collect taxes and supervise country estates, but as the authority of the shogun weakened, especially in eastern Japan, the military power and landed wealth of the *daimyō* grew. They began to behave like princes of independent states, promising to protect the local people, making their own laws, building castles, and creating castle towns that became centers of industry and commerce.

*Himeji Castle was originally built in the 14th century but was greatly enlarged in the Tokugawa Period. It is often called the White Heron, because its walls are plastered with white clay.*

almost completely destroyed. Under the weak and extravagant Ashikaga Yoshimasa (1435–1490), central government collapsed and the local warlords, called *daimyō* (see box), led Japan into the Period of the Warring States.

The Period of the Warring States was a time of universal warfare, when even warriors of low status raised armies and set themselves up as warlords. Rank and authority were ignored. Treachery and greed were the order of the day. In the middle of this terrible bloodshed, most of the old warrior families were destroyed. By 1560 the war had become a contest between the armies of a handful of powerful families. It was at this point that three outstanding leaders appeared to reunify the country.

## THREE POWERFUL MEN

The three men who finally brought stability and peace to Japan had very different characters. It is said that if a nightingale refused to sing, the first, Oda Nobunaga (1534–1582), would have killed it; the second, Toyotomi Hideyoshi (1539–1598), would have forced it; and the third, Tokugawa Ieyasu (1543–1616), would have waited.

Nobunaga was only the son of a minor samurai, but his ruthlessness enabled him to subdue almost one-third of all Japan in 20 years. His slogan was "Rule the country by force." In 1568 he captured Kyoto. The shogun Yoshiaki was deposed in 1573, finally abdicating in 1588. Nobunaga's most infamous act is the destruction of Enryakuji Temple. The fierce warrior-monks of this temple opposed Nobunaga, so he ordered his army to set fire to the temple and slaughter every one of the 20,000 men, women, and children inside. Yet he was also a great patron of the arts. He was hosting a tea ceremony at Azuchi Castle in 1582 when the castle was attacked. Nobunaga committed suicide to avoid death at the hands of his enemies.

**A CLOSER LOOK**

**The Japanese called muskets *tanegashima* because they were first brought to Tanegashima Island by the Portuguese in 1543.** **(See page 40.)** **The Japanese soon taught themselves how to manufacture muskets. They were first used with a considerable effect by Nobunaga's force of 3,000 against the combined armies of the Takeda clan at Nagashino in 1575. Nobunaga lined his musketeers up in three ranks, and the volleys of musket balls coming every ten seconds soon destroyed all opposition. Production of muskets became a thriving industry, even in temples, revolutionizing Japanese warfare.**

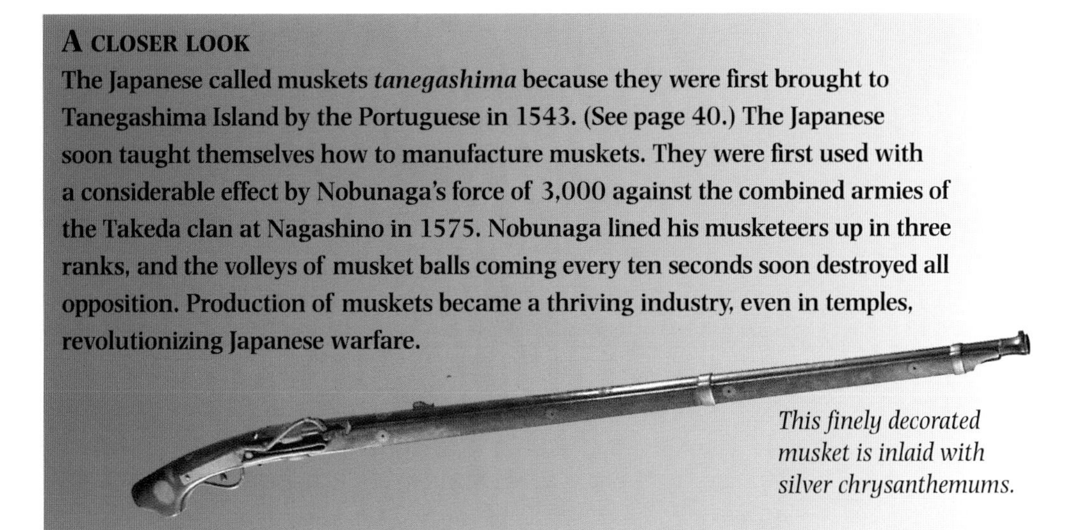

*This finely decorated musket is inlaid with silver chrysanthemums.*

His successor in the work of unification was Toyotomi Hideyoshi, who soon became regent to the emperor. Although he started his career as a humble foot soldier, he conquered the rest of Japan, and his armies even undertook an unsuccessful invasion of Korea. Hideyoshi is famous for his promotion of the tea ceremony, and he loved to demonstrate his power and wealth by building splendid castles—all of which were destroyed within a few years.

Soon after Hideyoshi died, the third powerful leader, Tokugawa Ieyasu, defeated his supporters at Sekigahara (1600), one of the most famous battles in Japanese history. Ieyasu already dominated eastern Japan, and when he became shogun in 1603, he chose to establish his headquarters in the east, at Edo (modern-day Tokyo). He had been a strong general even under Nobunaga, but, by waiting for the right opportunity, he eventually succeeded in unifying and ruling the whole country.

**A CLOSER LOOK**
**In 1588, in order to control the provinces and prevent any more civil wars, Hideyoshi ordered a "sword-hunt." All farmers had to hand in their swords and other weapons, and warriors were forced to leave the countryside and go to live in castle towns. For the first time, there was a strict division between warriors and the other classes. Hideyoshi also carried out a countrywide land survey and reorganized taxation. Later, the Tokugawa shoguns built on these reforms to set up a peaceful social order.**

## GROWING WEALTH

In spite of the Muromachi civil wars, the 16th century was an active period for trade and travel both within the country and overseas. The Japanese traded with China and Southeast Asia, and European merchants and missionaries arrived in Japan. (See Chapter 7.) Kyoto was one of the world's largest cities with a population of about 200,000. (London had about 50,000 inhabitants at this time.) The number of guilds grew, producing food such as noodles, fish products, and candy. There were craftsworkers' guilds for everything from silk and leather to bamboo and sickles.

Moneylenders and merchants were busier than ever. Records from 1460 show that in one small area of Kyoto carpenters, keg makers, smiths, *tatami* mat makers, and Buddhist statue makers were at work. There were also shops selling rice, rice cakes, *saké*, brooms, combs, needles, dyes, oils, and threads. The pattern was repeated around the country where many new towns, especially ports such as Sakai on the Inland Sea, grew rapidly. New roads made transportation and exchange of goods even easier. Silver mines, which increased the country's wealth, were discovered in about 1530. The wars actually promoted domestic trade and production, especially in arms and armor, including the newly introduced muskets. (See box page 23.) Castle-building projects gave work to thousands of stonemasons and carpenters, besides artists and specialist craftsworkers employed by the *daimyō*. These specialists competed with each other in displays of wealth.

Much of the growing prosperity depended on the continued efforts of many of the farmers who made up about 80 percent of the population. They grew better crops and became steadily richer, while providing merchants with more goods to sell. Peasants had more freedom to travel, visiting markets or setting out on pilgrimages—which were often no more than an excuse to have a good time!

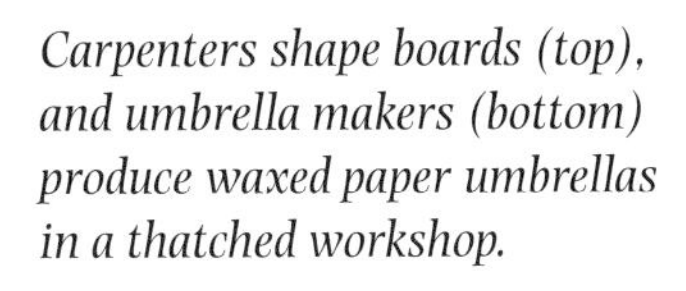

*Carpenters shape boards (top), and umbrella makers (bottom) produce waxed paper umbrellas in a thatched workshop.*

# THE TOKUGAWA SHOGUNATE

Tokugawa Ieyasu made his new capital in Edo (present-day Tokyo) and took the title of shogun in 1603. He established his authority once and for all in 1615 by killing Hideyoshi's son and his supporters at the siege of Osaka castle. Altogether, the Tokugawa family ruled for 15 generations and 264 years—the Edo Period. They enforced the class system, and for over two centuries after 1639 there were tight controls on Japan's contact with the outside world. A richly distinctive culture developed in relative peace, and Edo Period Japan is often described as "Traditional Japan."

## TOKUGAWA RULE

Ieyasu immediately set the tone for strict rule. There were about 260 *daimyō*. Most of these were from families who had come to power during the civil wars. The shogun divided them into three groups:

**A CLOSER LOOK**

**Rice had three main functions: it was the staple diet, it was widely used for payments instead of money, and it was used to measure the value of land. Using Hideyoshi's land surveys of the late 1580s, Ieyasu had each domain valued according to how many *koku* of rice it could produce in one year. A *koku* was enough rice to feed one person for a year. To qualify as a *daimyō*, a samurai had to control land valued at at least 10,000 *koku*. Ieyasu and his relatives controlled land worth seven million *koku*.**

*A modern farmhouse looks out over a newly planted rice field in northern Japan.*

*A grand* daimyō *procession crosses Nihombashi Bridge in Edo at the start of the Tōkaidō Road. Mount Fuji and Edo Castle can be seen in the background. The busy commercial life of the Sumida River is also shown, with barges carrying goods and storehouses lining the riverbanks.*

his relatives, allies, and former enemies. He and his family owned about one-third of the land. His loyal followers were placed in the Edo area or in regions that were important for defense or trade. Less trustworthy lords were placed on the fringes of the country surrounded by supporters of Ieyasu. The land entrusted to each *daimyō* was called a "domain."

The shogunate declared that "throughout the country all matters are to be carried out in accordance with the laws of Edo." All *daimyō* had to take an oath of loyalty, and if one of them rebelled, the shogun confiscated his land and gave it to another supporter. However, within their domains *daimyō* had a certain amount of authority, and the Tokugawa regime is sometimes called "shared government" between shogun and *daimyō*. Farmers had more security because the *daimyō* held fixed registers of each peasant's lands and collected taxes at an agreed rate.

From 1635 the shogunate enforced *daimyō* obedience in a cunning way. The *daimyō* were ordered to spend every other year in Edo and, when they returned to their domains, they had to leave their wives and children behind as hostages. The expense of maintaining two homes and organizing impressive processions back and forth meant that they did not have any spare money to start rebellions. *Daimyō* also had to give military service and supplies. In times of peace they provided materials and labor for the shogun's building projects. They were not allowed to extend their castles or build ocean-going ships, nor were their daughters allowed to marry without the shogun's permission.

**A CLOSER LOOK**
**During the Tokugawa Shogunate, the population was divided by law into four classes: samurai, farmers, craftsworkers, and merchants. The three lower classes—the commoners—had to serve the samurai and aristocracy. The merchants were placed last because they produced no food or goods and their work consisted only of buying and selling. Priests and nuns, doctors, teachers, and entertainers formed separate groups. There was also a class of people who were treated as outcasts, because the work they did was considered dirty or unpleasant.**

There was also strict control over Buddhist priests. The temples became important centers for the registration of people living in their area, but the religious practices of Buddhism gradually lost their influence. Shogun Hidetada was so confident of his position that, in 1615, he even passed laws limiting the activities of the emperor to poetry writing and Confucian studies. Officers supervised the emperor's court from Nijō Castle in Kyoto. This castle is famous for its "Nightingale Corridor," with floorboards designed to squeak a warning at the approach of an enemy.

## THE CITY OF EDO

One of the main features of the Edo Period was the growth of cities. By the end of the 18th century, Edo itself had a population of over a million people, probably the largest city in the world at that time, while Osaka and Kyoto each had populations of about 300,000. The reason why Edo was so large was that it was a garrison town—a town of warriors. At any one time, half the country's *daimyō* were staying there with their families and retainers. They all needed food, clothes, luxury goods, houses, entertainment, and religious ceremonies, so

*A group delivering fish in their thonged, straw sandals gather at the foot of Nihombashi Bridge in Edo.*

merchants, builders, artists, craftsworkers, and priests gathered in the city to work for them. In 1826, Philip von Siebold, a German doctor working for the Dutch merchants, described "the wide, busy streets bursting with sumptuous shops on either side." He also mentions several items that were relatively new introductions, including books, maps, woodblock prints, thin glass containers, tobacco pipes, tortoise-shell hairpins, and children's toys. The streets of Edo were always teeming with life as jugglers, tumblers, and musicians entertained those who passed by.

Edo was a large castle town, with a central keep surrounded by mansions for *daimyō* and their followers. Beyond these was the vast network of shops and workshops. Great temples guarded each corner. Edo had a good, clean water supply. Rings of canals gave extra defense and also helped to stop fires from spreading. Fire towers were a familiar sight, and firemen had their own guild. Even so, the Great Meireki Fire of 1657 destroyed most of the city.

## SHOGUNS AND THE FOREIGNERS

When Ieyasu Tokugawa became shogun in 1603, Japan was trading widely with many Asian

**A CLOSER LOOK**

**The Tokugawa shoguns established a network of roads which all led to Edo. There was no wheeled traffic, so the roads were unpaved. Important people were carried in palanquins, while everybody else went on horseback or on foot. The most famous of the new roads was the Tōkaidō, "East Sea Road," which followed the coast from Edo to Kyoto. There were 53 stations where travelers could rest and change their horses. There were also barriers, such as Hakone, where *daimyō* processions were inspected for guns going into Edo, or women being smuggled out!**

countries. Portuguese and Spanish merchants and missionaries had been there since the previous century, and the Dutch had recently arrived. However, the missionaries and their Japanese Christian converts had already fallen out of favor with Hideyoshi, and Ieyasu and his successors continued to persecute them. The shoguns were afraid that the Christian belief in one God could weaken their own authority. They also suspected that the European missionaries and merchants might be seeking help from the Japanese Christians to take over Japan as a colony. This had already happened in Mexico and the Philippines.

As a result of these fears, the shogunate banned Christianity and forced all missionaries from the country. In addition, no Japanese citizens were allowed to enter or leave Japan. Finally, in 1639, the Portuguese merchants were expelled. Only the Chinese and the Dutch (who did not teach Christianity) were allowed to stay and trade—under strict supervision. (See page 41.)

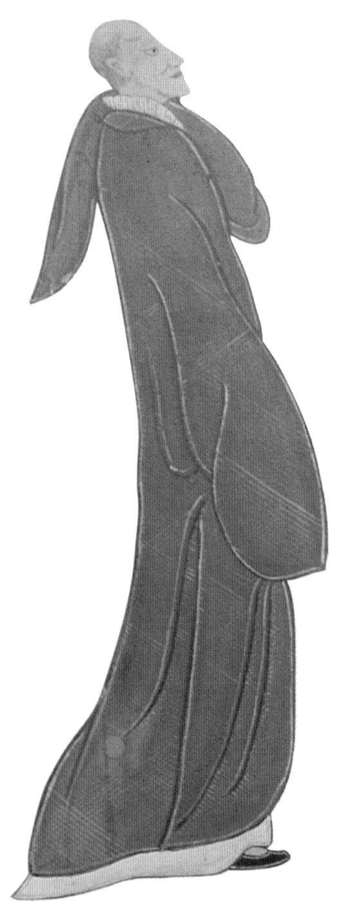

*The Japanese were fascinated by the strange appearance of these tall Portuguese priests, with their long noses and flowing robes.*

## DECLINE AND FALL

For two centuries the Tokugawa shoguns were successful in keeping the country peaceful and the people contented. However, from the early 1800s, they were faced with three kinds of problems that finally led to their downfall. First, there were natural disasters—earthquakes, volcanic eruptions, and famines—which caused thousands of deaths. Secondly, the spread of business and trade opened

*Commodore Perry sailed into Uraga Bay with his threatening Black Ships. The samurai, fearful yet curious, flocked out in small boats for a closer look.*

up a wide gap between rich and poor. Many samurai fell into debt through living luxuriously, and relations between the central government and the domains gradually grew worse. The third problem came from outside, as foreign ships started to sail threateningly into Japanese waters.

The big test came in 1853, when Commodore Matthew Perry, an American, sailed into Uraga Bay with three warships. He demanded diplomatic relations with Japan and returned for shogun Iesada's answer in 1854. Realizing that resistance was useless, Iesada was forced to accept Perry's demands. Iesada later signed trade treaties with the United States, in addition to the Netherlands, Britain, France, and Russia. Once again, foreigners began to establish settlements on Japanese soil.

The 1860s was a time of uncertainty. The shogun seemed incapable of defending the country. A group of leading samurai formed an alliance, believing that only the authority of the emperor could save Japan at this critical time. They finally succeeded in abolishing the shogunate and restoring the emperor to power in 1868. This event in Japan's history is called the Meiji Restoration. (See pages 57–59.)

# The World of the Samurai

The missionary, Francis Xavier (see page 40), described the Japanese as the most warlike race he had ever met. Indeed, the ruling warrior class, the samurai, lived their lives in the constant expectation of war and death. But they still found time for the appreciation of beauty in the quiet arts of Zen and the sumptuous decoration of their castles.

## Who were the samurai?

An elite class of warriors called samurai was created by the emperor in the late 8th century to fight the tribes in northern Japan. From the early 10th century, the samurai leaders began to take control in many areas of Japan. They rose to power because the central government of the emperor and courtiers in Kyoto took little interest in provincial affairs. As central authority weakened, the ambitions of the samurai leaders grew. They seized lands and formed armies to protect their estates. Most of them were gentlemen farmers who worked the land between campaigns.

Samurai means "one who serves," and these leaders demanded total loyalty from their followers, known as "vassals," who regarded their lords almost as fathers. The top samurai leaders were from the Taira and

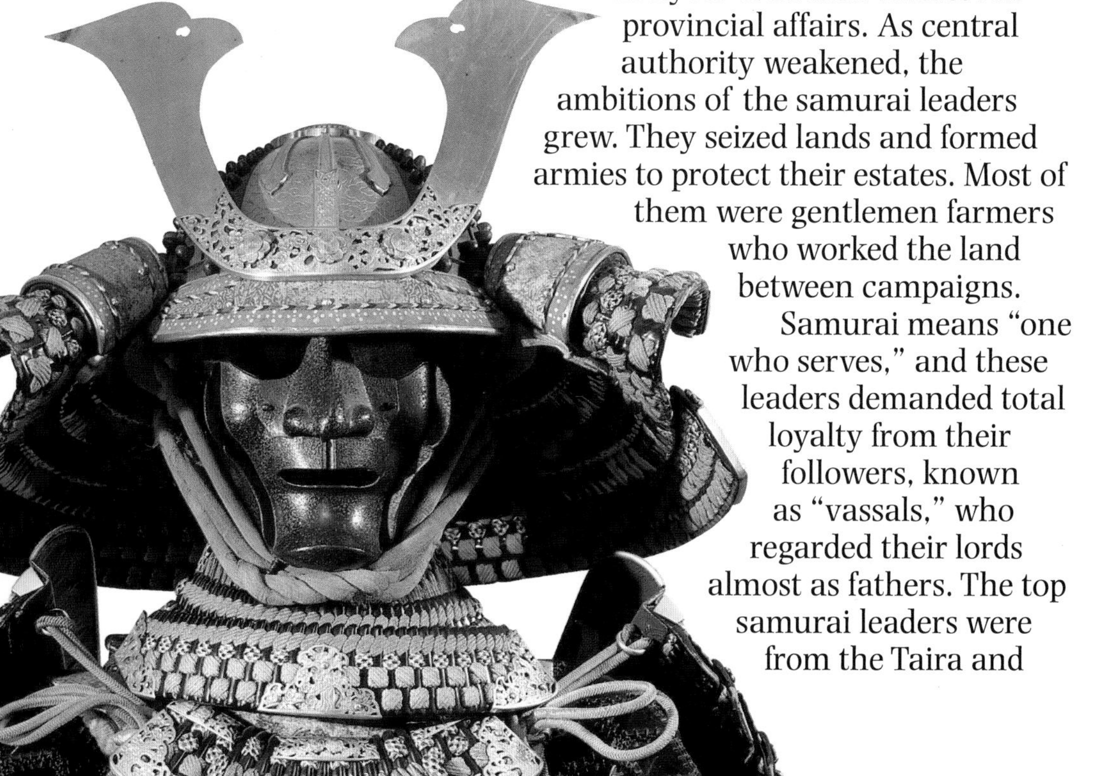

*Samurai warriors wore helmets with horns and terrifying masks to strike fear into their enemies. In this picture you can see that the lacquered scales of armor are held together with silk cords.*

Minamoto families. They were distantly related to the imperial line and were therefore highly respected. The emperor had to rely on them to put down serious rebellions that spread to Kyoto itself in the 1150s, so the Taira and Minamoto became involved in court politics. Finally, they challenged each other in the Gempei Wars. (See page 13.) The victor, Minamoto Yoritomo, became military ruler of the whole country, and the samurai were feared and respected as the ruling class for 700 years.

## THE SAMURAI UNDER THE SHOGUNS

There were strict ranks within the samurai class that were passed down from father to son. At the top was the shogun, next came his government officials, then the provincial lords, and last their vassals. The system worked as long as the shogun was strong. However, under the weak 15th-century shoguns, the lower ranks rose against their superiors and civil war engulfed the country in the Period of the Warring States. (See page 22.) The samurai were constantly occupied in fighting, but their ideals of loyalty and honor were almost forgotten.

After the reunification of Japan at the end of the 16th century, the samurai were in a strange position because there were no wars to fight, and they were not allowed to be farmers. Forced to live in castle towns, many of them became government officials. They continued to wear two swords in public to remind people that the military were in charge. There was not enough work for them all, so many samurai spent their time looking for amusement—or trouble.

**A CLOSER LOOK**

**There were many masterless samurai called *rōnin*. Their lords had lost their lands as punishment. Some *rōnin* became aimless troublemakers, but others were monks, teachers, or craftsworkers, or practiced the martial arts. Miyamoto Musashi (1584–1645) fought on the losing side at the Battle of Sekigahara in 1600. As a *rōnin*, he decided to perfect the art of *kendō*. By the age of 30 he had fought 60 single combat sword fights, killing his opponent every time. He wrote a *kendō* handbook called *A Book of Five Rings*. To some people he may appear pitiless and cruel, yet the Japanese call him Kensei, "Sword Saint," and admire him for his devotion to his ideals.**

In this time of peace, some warriors remembered their past as a golden age. In 1665, Yamaga Sokō wrote a book about samurai ideals called *The Way of the Warrior.* Yamaga reminded warriors to live frugally and to practice the martial arts, especially *kendō*, the "Way of the Sword," in preparation for death. Many samurai remained true to their old ideals. After the shogunate fell in 1868, and the samurai class was abolished, some of these men, with their clear-headedness and strength of character, became the new leaders of Japan.

## ARMS, ARMOR, AND BATTLES

The samurai's chief weapons were the bow; the sword; the halberd, or spear; and later, the musket and cannon. Bows were taller than a person, and mounted archers had to shoot arrows with deadly accuracy while galloping at full speed.

*The sword-polisher, Ken Mishina, demonstrates that his art lives on in modern-day Japan.*

The long sword was the samurai's most prized possession, described by Ieyasu as "the soul of the samurai." Swords were forged in great secrecy with much ceremony. Swordsmiths were the most revered of all artisans, sometimes engraving their signature on the blades they made. They developed techniques of beating and folding the steel to produce a hard but flexible blade with a shallow curve and a razor-sharp cutting edge. Swords were also admired for their beauty. The beating and folding produced a fine wave pattern along the edge. Swordguards and scabbards were decorated with birds and flowers. Each sword had an awe-inspiring spirit of its own, so it had to be treated with great care by its owner and never drawn without just cause.

Full armor consisted of at least 23 different items. Body armor was made of leather or lacquered metal scales strung together with colored silk braids, while the fearsome helmets and masks were designed to strike terror into the enemy. Japanese armor changed as weapons and ways of fighting changed. Warriors needed greater protection and more mobility on foot.

Up to the end of the 15th century, there were strict rules for battles. Leaders on each side agreed on the time and place. The action consisted largely of single combat. Each warrior rode forward loudly boasting his family connections and brave deeds until he found a rival of equal status. The fight was always to the death. When a combatant fell, his rival would dismount, kill him, and cut off his head. Every fighter made sure that his deeds were noticed by his lord, so that he would be well rewarded. Once the enemy had been defeated, the victors slaughtered all the survivors to prevent revenge attacks. However, during the Period of Warring States, samurai codes of combat were forgotten. Then surprise attacks, fighting between men of all ranks, and large-scale maneuvers became the rule.

**A CLOSER LOOK**
**The most dreaded punishment for an archer was to have his drawing finger cut off. This happened to Minamoto Tametomo, one of the most celebrated bowmen in Japanese history, when he was captured by his enemy, the Taira. In this picture (right) he is shown with four mythical Japanese demons who are straining in vain to draw his bow.**

## ZEN AND ZEN ARTS

Zen Buddhism was brought from China by Japanese monks and practiced by the Kamakura shoguns and samurai from the 12th century onward. With its new values and cultural traditions, it appealed to the samurai. Zen also brought with it some of the glory and power of the Chinese court, which enhanced the prestige of the shogunate.

Zen means "meditation." The practice of Zen consists of sitting motionless with legs crossed, emptying the mind of all desire and anxiety. Zen Buddhists try to reach self-understanding and tranquillity through their own efforts. This requires discipline, a simple way of life, and an iron will. Zen

### A CLOSER LOOK

**Zen arts were usually enjoyed by the samurai in private. But, when they wanted to show off their position in public, they chose a completely different style. Sets of huge folding screens, or whole rooms were painted in grandiose manner to celebrate their owner's wealth and power. Hideyoshi (see page 24) covered the entire top story of a castle in goldleaf. He even owned a teahouse and set of tea utensils that were made entirely of gold.**

*This impressive screen may have been displayed by Hideyoshi himself at his military headquarters. Chinese lions symbolized power and bravery.*

suited the samurai who trained themselves to fight with no thought of victory or defeat, life or death.

The warriors also favored the quiet, harmonious Zen arts that stressed the importance of the present moment and contrasted with the brutality of the battlefield. Calligraphy and paintings were executed with a few swift brushstrokes. Flower arrangements consisted of a handful of carefully chosen blooms representing Heaven, Earth, and Man. Temple gardens often contained only sand and stones, carefully arranged to look like a landscape. Buildings were plain but elegant.

Above all, the tea ceremony, which started as a samurai pastime, has influenced nearly every aspect of Japanese culture since the 15th century. In a tea ceremony, two or three people are invited by their host to eat a special meal and drink powdered green tea prepared according to strict rules in a tiny rustic teahouse. The Ashikaga shoguns were devoted to the tea ceremony, and so was Hideyoshi. (See page 24.) Hideyoshi's tea master, Sen no Rikyū (1521–1591), founded one of the schools of tea in Kyoto where the tea ceremony is still taught. Rikyū described the tea ceremony as a time for simplicity, respect, service, and harmony: "The tea person draws water, gathers firewood, and boils water. He makes tea, offers it to the Buddha, serves it to others, and last, he too drinks."

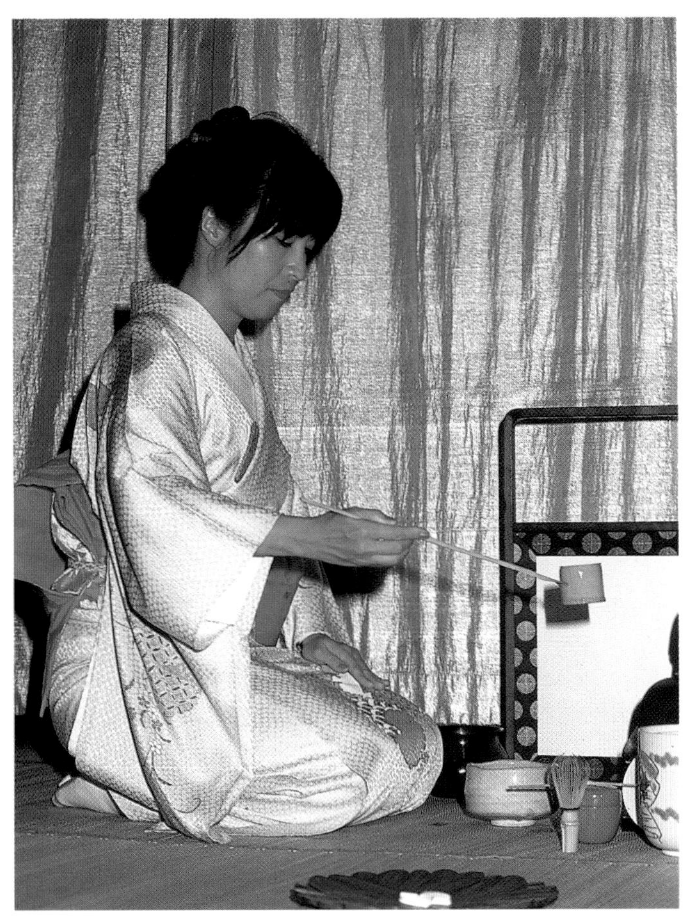

*In this tea ceremony, the host is pouring hot water onto powdered green tea. The tea will be mixed with the bamboo whisk (front right) and offered to a guest.*

# Japan and the Outside World

The earliest Japanese maps of the world show only Buddhist countries—China and India with Japan in the middle. Beyond that were regions that people believed were inhabited by monsters and demons. But when Europeans reached Japan in the 16th century, they brought maps from which the Japanese learned more about distant places. The Japanese copied Dutch maps and later made up-to-date maps of their own.

*The Japanese prized Chinese porcelain, such as this 15th-century stem cup, until the beginning of the 17th century when they learned to make porcelain for themselves.*

## Japan and China

For over 2,000 years, China was the most advanced country in the world and demanded obedience from surrounding states, including Korea and Japan. The Japanese remained independent from China but always had a strong admiration for Chinese culture. They continued to seek trade and cultural contacts until the middle of the 19th century.

During the Kamakura Period, the Hōjō regents became enthusiastic collectors of elegant Chinese works of art. They also welcomed Zen Buddhism, and Japanese and Chinese Zen monks. Merchants traveled frequently between the two countries. The Mongol invasions interrupted these links for a while, but voyages back and forth started up again by the end of the 13th century.

China was at peace under the Ming emperors (1368–1644). During this time the Muromachi shogun, Yoshimitsu, established successful diplomatic and trade ties. However, after the fall of the Muromachi Shogunate, peaceful relations with China suddenly came to a halt when the Japanese warlord, Hideyoshi, invaded China's ally, Korea in both 1592 and 1597. This was the first step in Hideyoshi's plan to become master of Asia. But his armies were turned back, and Hideyoshi died, bringing the war effort to an end. China and Korea became Japan's bitter enemies.

The first Tokugawa shogun, Ieyasu, tried to reestablish diplomatic and trade relations with China. The Chinese refused, but Ieyasu encouraged private trading that continued under the Vermilion Seal system (see box) until it was stopped by Iemitsu in 1639. After this, Chinese merchants, were allowed to stay on in Nagasaki only, and Chinese junks sailed in regularly bringing silks and spices, medicines and books that they exchanged for precious metals.

**A CLOSER LOOK**

**During the late 16th and early 17th centuries, many Japanese merchants set sail from the port of Sakai to trade in Southeast Asia, in today's Thailand, Vietnam, and Cambodia, Luzon in the Philippines, and Taiwan. They established "Japanese towns" in several places. These towns were half-way houses where they met Chinese traders to obtain silk. Ieyasu encouraged this trade by issuing special licenses to certain merchants. These licenses were stamped with his bright vermilion seal to prove they were genuine, and to guarantee the merchants' safety on their voyages.**

Chinese influence continued in other ways. Confucianism emphasized obedience and loyalty, and it strongly influenced Tokugawa political ideas and samurai life. The Tokugawa class system of "samurai-farmer-craftsworker-merchant" (see page 28) was based on Chinese Confucian models. A new Chinese Zen sect was introduced in 1654, and imported books spread knowledge of painting, medicine, and astronomy. By the late 18th century, however, many Japanese began to renew their interest in their own history and native Shintō values. Others were seriously studying Western ideas. Centuries of Chinese influence ended when China was defeated by the British army and navy in 1842 and 1860. Then, Japan found itself forced to modernize in order to avoid a similar fate.

**A closer look**

**Francis Xavier described Japanese as "the language of the Devil." He meant that the strange language made it difficult for him to teach Christianity. Similarly, the Japanese were puzzled by European writing, comparing it with "wriggling earthworms moving sideways." But some Portuguese learned Japanese, and several Japanese later became fluent in Dutch. After 1868, however, English came into fashion and Dutch was rarely used.**

## The Europeans

Travelers from Portugal, Spain, the Netherlands, and England all reached Japan in the 16th century, but only the Dutch and Portuguese stayed on. The first European arrivals were some Portuguese sailors who were shipwrecked on the island of Tanegashima in 1543.

Merchants and missionaries soon followed, among them the great Catholic missionary, Francis Xavier, a Spaniard working for the Portuguese. He arrived in 1549, at the beginning of Japan's "Christian century." At first Nobunaga (see page 23) welcomed the Christian teachers, seeing them as useful allies against the troublesome Buddhist warrior-monks. The missionaries made many thousands of Christian converts mainly among the *daimyō* of Kyūshū and their vassals, and even built a church in Kyoto. Xavier liked the Japanese, admiring their "exceptionally fine manners." The Japanese called all foreigners "red-furred Southern Barbarians" and were fascinated by their strange appearance, their long noses, and baggy trousers. Portuguese merchants were given permission to trade from Nagasaki harbor, and every year a Portuguese ship arrived bringing Chinese silk from Macao, an island near Hong Kong, to exchange for Japanese silver.

When the first Dutch ship, the *Liefde*, reached the Japanese coast on April 19, 1600, the Portuguese wanted Ieyasu to kill the sailors. They thought that the Dutch might steal their trade, which is exactly what happened. Not only was Ieyasu impressed by the Dutch firearms, but he also noted that the Dutch did not preach Christianity, which by then was becoming unpopular in Japan. Iesayu invited the Dutch to make a trade treaty.

Over the following decades, Portuguese trade and popularity weakened as suspicion of the missionaries

*This painted screen shows Portuguese merchants in enormous baggy trousers sailing into Nagasaki harbor, bringing all sorts of exotic goods.*

and Christians grew. (See page 30.) Many executions took place and Japanese converts were forced to give up their new faith and register as Buddhists. Finally, an armed uprising by Japanese Christians at Shimabara in Kyūshū caused the shogun, Iemitsu, to ban Christianity in Japan, and all the Portuguese were banished. From 1639, only Chinese and Dutch merchants were allowed to stay and trade, and the Dutch became the most important European influence in Japan for the next 250 years.

## DUTCH LEARNING

Besides trading with Japan throughout the Edo Period, the Dutch provided information about the outside world and Western science. The Deshima captain and his senior staff (see box page 42) had to visit Edo regularly to honor the shogun and present gifts—silk, spices, even camels and an ostrich. The shoguns took this opportunity to question the foreigners. One of the staff, a doctor named Engelbert Kaempfer, who lived in Japan 1690–1692, described in detail how the shogun commanded them to dance, sing, and act foolishly. He wrote an account

**A CLOSER LOOK**

**The Japanese were suspicious of the Dutch because—although they did not teach Christianity—they still practiced their religion publicly. The Dutch were ordered to stop all Christian worship and, from 1541, the merchants and their staff were forced to live on a tiny, human-made island called Deshima, in Nagasaki Bay. It was like a prison, only 590 feet (180 m) long and 197 feet (60 m) wide, surrounded by a fence of sharpened stakes. The Dutch complained bitterly, but trade flourished. Between 1541 and 1847 a total of 606 Dutch ships visited Nagasaki.**

*This painting shows life on Deshima. Upstairs (right) some Dutchmen are dining. Next door, tea is served to a Japanese official, while musicians play European stringed instruments.*

of his experiences that was translated into English and published in London in 1727. It was the first important European history of Japan.

Some Japanese were eager for more serious studies in medicine and physics. Another Deshima doctor, Philip von Siebold, who lived in Japan 1823–1830, taught medicine in Nagasaki and Edo. In 1771, Sugita Gempaku and three friends became the first Japanese to watch the dissection of a human corpse. They realized that their Chinese textbooks were wildly inaccurate, and they painstakingly translated a Dutch anatomy textbook. Interest also grew in many other subjects. A group of *daimyō* studied natural history and made detailed drawings of plants, animals, and insects. Previously they had discovered from the Chinese how to use plants as medicines. Now they learned in Dutch books how to divide them into groups according to Western science. In the world of art, a few Japanese artists experimented with Western perspective and techniques of light and shade. In Edo there was an eager exchange of knowledge between *daimyō*, who then took the new ideas back to their domains.

## FOREIGNERS IN YOKOHAMA

After the Americans made their treaties with Japan (see page 31), Britain, the Netherlands, France, and Russia also made treaties of trade and friendship. From 1859, much of the activity was centered in Yokohama near Edo. Most of the foreigners lived there, and it quickly became a large cosmopolitan city with Western-style brick buildings. Once again, the Japanese were faced with strangers bearing mysterious gifts. The shogun was presented with a model steam engine on which a samurai took a ride with his robes flying. But this was only a taste of things to come. After the restoration of the emperor's rule in 1868, the modernization of Japanese life along Western lines continued at breakneck speed.

*The Union Jack flag flies above the British headquarters in Yokohama. Even the picture title is given in English. In front of the new brick buildings, onlookers watch a Western-style military march led by a band.*

# Everyday Life

At the beginning of the Kamakura Period, there was a big gap between the rich and poor in terms of diet, clothing, housing, education, family life, and entertainment. As time passed, and farms and businesses expanded, some commoners began to lead more comfortable lives. In the Edo Period, many rich merchants could afford to live almost like samurai. Some of their traditional ways of life still survive in modern-day Japan.

*A busy scene at an inn. In the left-hand room, a waitress hands in two meals on separate lacquer tables. A guest lounges on the floor. On the veranda a guest arrives back from the bathhouse carrying his towel.*

## Food

The basic Japanese diet has remained the same from the Yayoi Period (300 B.C.–A.D. 300), through

**A CLOSER LOOK**
**Presentation of food has always been very important in Japan. At a meal, there could be five different containers—two covered bowls for rice and soup, and three others for fish and pickled vegetables. Each person had a separate tray or little table, laid with a pair of bamboo or lacquered chopsticks, a pottery chopstick rest, and a teacup without a handle.**

shogun times, and to the present day. It is very simple, based on rice and fish, with vegetables often gathered from the wilderness, such as bamboo shoots. The importance of rice is shown by the fact that *gohan*, the Japanese word for "rice" can also mean "food" or "a meal." Buddhism forbade the consumption of meat, but people sometimes ate wild boar, calling it "mountain whale." By the 14th century, soybean products, such as *tōfu* (beancurd), were common, while during the Edo Period, *sushi* (raw fish on rice) and Portuguese *tempura* (fish and vegetables fried in light batter) became popular. The production of *saké* (rice wine) started in the Yayoi Period. It was often drunk on ceremonial occasions. Green tea was the ordinary, everyday drink.

## CLOTHING

In the Kamakura Period, the dress for upper-class Japanese men and women was a loose robe made of silk worn over long trousers. All garments for both sexes crossed over from left to right. (Right over left is only for corpses.) There were different styles for ceremonial, court, and working clothes. As fashions changed, men wore their robes tucked into the trousers with a wide-shouldered jacket. For a time, men's ceremonial trousers were very long, covering the feet and trailing behind.

The Japanese kimono developed for everyday wear around the mid-16th century. Men's sashes were quite narrow, but women's sashes, called *obi*, became progressively wider and more decorative. These sashes were tied with a complicated bow, usually at the back. There was no jewelry, but women in the Edo Period wore elaborate hairpins and combs.

**A CLOSER LOOK**

**A kimono was made of wide strips of silk sewn together in a T-shape. Sometimes the silk had a pattern woven into it. Sometimes it was dyed, painted, or embroidered, often with gold and silver thread. In the late Edo Period, rich merchants' wives and daughters liked to wear these gorgeous silks. However, because merchants were in the lowest social class, the government tried to prohibit their extravagance by law. At such times minutely stenciled designs, stripes, and checks became the fashion.**

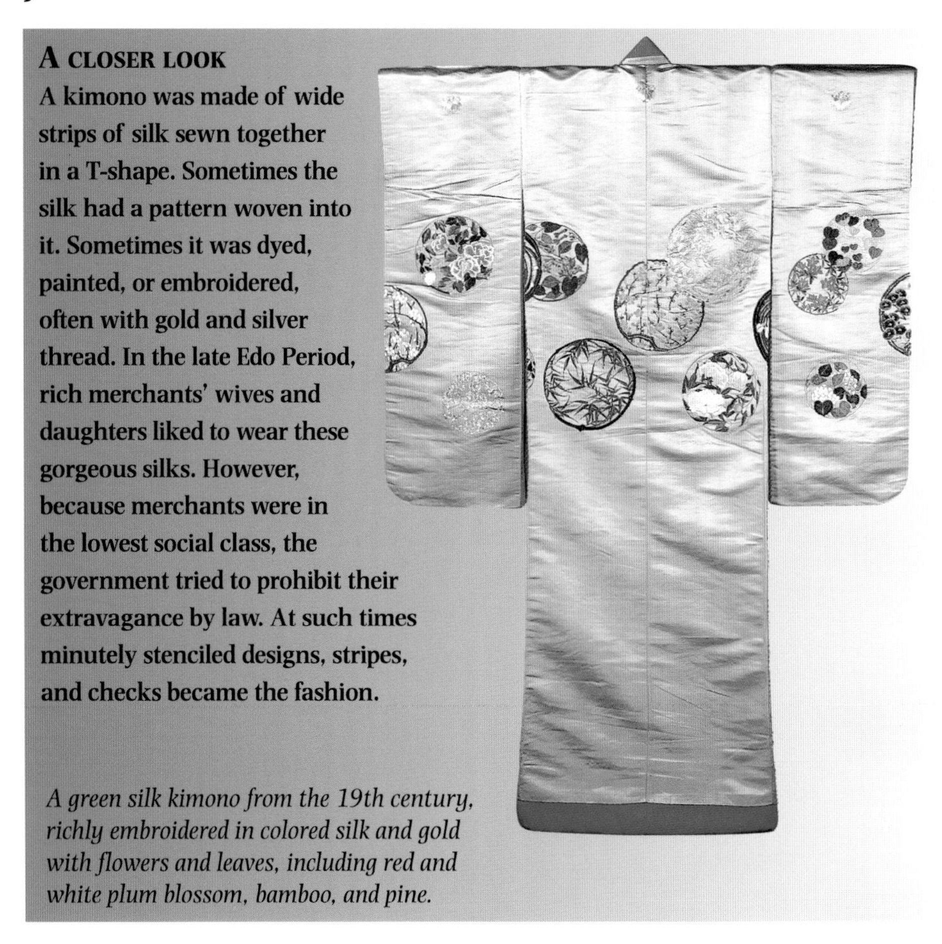

*A green silk kimono from the 19th century, richly embroidered in colored silk and gold with flowers and leaves, including red and white plum blossom, bamboo, and pine.*

They used white powder and lip rouge. When they came of age they shaved their eyebrows, painting them in high on the forehead. They also blackened their teeth because white teeth were considered unattractive. Merchant women blackened their teeth when they married.

Peasants of both sexes wore hemp or cotton trousers with a belted jacket. Shoes were made of straw or wood and had a thong which went between the big and second toes. Some shoes had high platform soles, so that the wearer could walk in muddy streets.

## HOUSES

Houses were built of wood using special techniques to prevent them collapsing during an earthquake. The main uprights were stood on carefully shaped stones, so that they could bounce, and the joints

*Many modern Japanese houses, like this one, have traditional features, such as overhanging eaves and sliding doors opening onto a raised veranda. Bedding hangs to air on an upper balcony. The Japanese-style garden has rocks and neatly trimmed trees.*

were very flexible. (Modern engineers have copied these ideas for earthquake-proof skyscrapers.) From the Heian Period, the Japanese stopped using chairs and other furniture and started living at floor level. In upper-class homes, the floors were covered with *tatami*, rice straw mats with a smooth surface of woven grass. Rooms were used for different purposes, furnished with cushions and low tables for daytime, while bedding was brought from small closets at night. In the main reception room, there was a beautifully made set of wooden shelves and an alcove, called a *tokonoma*, in which a fine scroll painting or an elegant flower arrangement could be displayed. Houses were built to be cool in summer rather than warm in winter, when everyone gathered around a central hearth or used charcoal-burning hand warmers. There was no glass, so that windows were tightly shuttered at night.

**A CLOSER LOOK**

**Japanese houses were raised on a platform, and hosts welcomed their guests with "Please step up," rather than "Please come in." Everyone removed outdoor shoes before entering. This is still the custom today.**

Farmers, fishermen, and artisans lived in simpler thatched houses with a dirt-floor working area and a sunken hearth for cooking and heating. Some farmhouses had a stable for a horse. Others were two-story buildings, with a room upstairs where silkworms were raised. Shopkeepers in the city of Edo lived in two-story townhouses with the shop opening onto the street and living quarters behind and above. Many buildings were plastered with clay to protect against fire.

## THE LIFE OF WOMEN

Japanese warrior society was male-dominated. In earlier periods, there were a few female rulers, and some women were allowed to inherit property. However, in the civil wars from the late Heian Period onward, it was thought necessary to have a man at the head of the family to protect the house and land.

Women had little freedom in their daily lives. Warlords sometimes married off their daughters to powerful neighbors simply to strengthen alliances. Women and even children were not spared from mass slaughter, and many wives committed suicide with their husbands.

The lives of lower-class women were also hard, though they probably had more freedom than noblewomen in their choice of husbands. Farmers' wives planted the rice and helped with tending the growing crop, besides cooking, spinning, weaving, and caring for their children. Poorer townsmen's wives helped their husbands with the family business and ran their homes. The wives of rich merchants were perhaps the best off. In spite of their low position in society, they had money and often led luxurious lives.

Very few women managed to become famous during their

**A CLOSER LOOK**

**In 1716, strict rules governing a woman's behavior according to Confucian laws were written down in a book called *The Great Learning for Women*. It was a woman's duty to obey her father, her husband, and her sons. A man could divorce his wife simply by sending her back to her parents saying she was unhealthy, she was unable to have children, or even just talked too much. For a woman, the only escape was to run away to a refuge temple and become a nun. There were very few of these temples, but if a woman stayed there for at least two years she could obtain a divorce.**

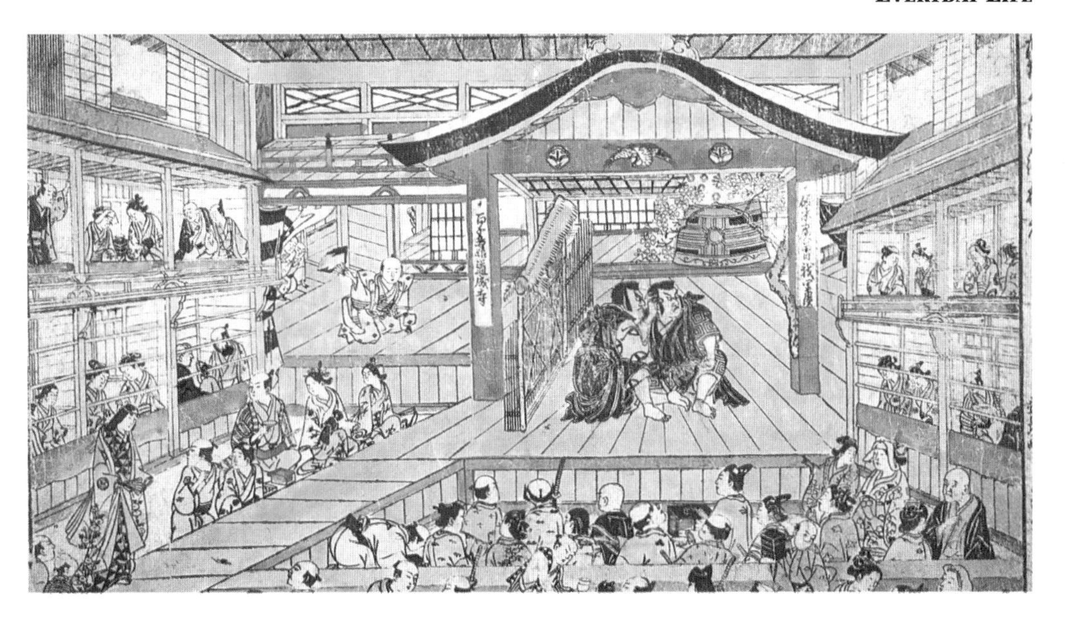

*Soon after open-air* kabuki *performances by women were banned, indoor theaters were built. Then, men started to play both male and female roles. Here, a female character approaches the stage along a walkway called a* hanamichi*—"flower-path."*

own lifetimes, but there were a few exceptions. One of the most well-known was the female entertainer Okuni who is said to have founded *kabuki* theater. (See page 56.) She performed with her female troupe in Kyoto. They caused such a sensation that they were banned in about 1629 for their bad influence on the townspeople.

## CHILDREN

Up to the age of seven, children were treated as infants and were rarely parted from their mothers. From seven years onward, they were seen as miniature adults. Boys and girls were separated and, depending on their class in society, they either received education or training, or started helping

**A CLOSER LOOK**

**Upper class women enjoyed the shell game, which was played with beautifully painted pairs of shells. (See page 10.) A poem was written, half on one shell, half on the other, and the game consisted of pairing up the shells to make a complete poem. Board games such as *go*, a game of strategy using small black and white disks, were also popular. During the Edo Period, children began to play with toys, such as spinning tops and toy tigers. At New Year, boys flew kites, and girls played an elegant form of badminton. In spring nearly everyone went to see the flowering cherry trees, which were often planted in temple grounds and parks.**

A kind elder sister changes the pictures in a new foreign toy, for her two little brothers. Inside the box a series of lenses threw an image on to a screen at the back.

with their parents' farm or store. Older girls looked after the younger children. Under the Kamakura and Ashikaga shoguns, most samurai boys studied Chinese in the domain schools, while their sisters were educated at home to be hardworking, obedient wives. Some commoners' children attended elementary schools called *terakoya*. In the Edo Period, samurai boys had to study Confucian laws, while commoners' children concentrated on reading, writing, and arithmetic using the *soroban* (abacus). By 1868, 15 percent of boys could read and write, more than in most other countries at that time.

## FESTIVALS

New Year was the most important festival of the year, but there were many other festivals when hard-working commoners could enjoy themselves. Many of the country festivals were Shintō ceremonies to bless the fields at different seasons. The Bon Odori Lantern Festival was held in autumn. People believed that the spirits of their ancestors visited the village to ensure a good harvest. They lit paper lanterns and danced with great energy to entertain these spirits. Children had their own festivals, too. For the Boys' Festival on May 5, models of samurai armor were put on show, and parents prayed that their sons would have the courage to face life's problems. Girls' Day on March 3 was celebrated by displaying dolls dressed as the emperor, empress, and courtiers.

# Art, Literature, and Entertainment

*This wooden statue is one of a pair of Guardian Kings at the gateway to Nakayamadera Temple in Fukui Prefecture. The statues' fierce expressions protect Buddhism from evil.*

Japan under the shoguns was a place of great energy and perfectionism in every aspect of the arts. Painters, sculptors and potters, writers, actors, and musicians all worked in the service of samurai and rich merchants. During the Edo Period, society was strictly divided, but samurai and townspeople often shared the same tastes and met at theaters, sumō wrestling matches, and poetry and painting events.

## Sculptures Large and Small

The Kamakura Period (1185–1333) was the high point of Japanese wood sculpture. During the Gempei Wars, many important temples and their treasures were destroyed by fire, so Minamoto Yoritomo commissioned sculptors, led by Unkei, to make replacements. With his assistants, Unkei produced figures of Buddhas, guardian deities, rulers, and priests. Earlier sculptors had used only one piece of wood, but Unkei carved the limbs separately before fixing them to the body, so that statues could take on more dramatic poses. The expressions of the statues were made more lifelike with the use of real crystal for the eyes.

In complete contrast to these huge works, were the tiny carved toggles (holding devices) called *netsuke*, often made of ivory, which became popular about 400 years later in the Edo Period. Men hung small medicine boxes called *inrō*, on cords threaded through their sashes, and *netsuke* were used to keep the boxes in place. *Netsuke* took many forms—animals, insects, mythical beasts, and Chinese sages. These tiny carvings could fit into the palm of the hand, but every detail was perfect. They were often worn by merchants to display their wealth.

*This ivory mouse* netsuke *is slightly more than 2 inches (5.5 cm) long.*

## Pottery and porcelain

Japanese pottery has perhaps the longest tradition in the world, going back to 10,000 B.C. The first pots were serviceable, everyday ware. Their beauty was in the patterns that formed accidentally in the kiln—scorch-marks, patterns of burned straw and flecks of ash. In the early days of the tea ceremony, the Ashikaga shoguns preferred to use Chinese porcelain. However, as the tea ceremony became a more simple, private event in a rustic teahouse, tea masters found the imperfect shapes and natural colors of Japanese pots more suitable. Korean rice bowls were also prized as tea bowls. After Hideyoshi's unsuccessful invasions of Korea in the 1590s, many Korean potters were brought back to Japan as prisoners. Their work was soon in demand, especially in Kyūshū. The Koreans also taught the Japanese how to make delicately patterned porcelain that was soon used throughout the country as crockery for everyday use. Much Japanese porcelain found its way into the palaces of Europe, imported by Dutch merchants.

## Official painters

Under the shoguns, different groups, or "schools," of painters existed side-by-side working in varying styles. Each school had its master who passed his title on to his son or an outstanding pupil. The

**A CLOSER LOOK**
Japanese art often has hidden meanings: bamboo and tigers signify strength; cranes are for long life. A very popular subject is a scene of irises growing by a bridge. This scene refers to a famous story from the Heian Period which tells how some travelers, far from home, sat by a bridge over a pool where irises were in bloom and wrote poems about their loved ones back in Kyoto. They started to cry into their rice bowls, making the grains of rice swell up. Ever since, irises have always reminded the Japanese of absent friends. On the right is part of a famous version of this scene painted by Sakai Hōitsu (1761–1828) on two large screens.

imperial family favored the Tosa School that depicted scenes of the Japanese seasons and countryside, festivals, and court ceremonies. The shoguns chose the Kanō School, which dominated Japanese painting for nearly 400 years from the late 1400s. The artist's duty was to glorify his patron, producing grand-scale, ceremonial works. Master painters employed teams of pupils to help paint these large-scale works. Since they had all learned to imitate his style, the final painting looked as if it had been done by a single painter.

Artists also painted the sliding doors and six-fold screens used to divide rooms and keep out drafts. They often chose themes from nature and the changing seasons. Sometimes they used gold leaf, which glowed in the candlelight, brightening up the dim interiors of castles and temples. Paintings on silk were mounted on hanging scrolls that were changed with the seasons. These hanging scrolls, often in sets of three, were hung in the *tokonoma* alcoves (see page 47) of samurai mansions.

Ghosts and grotesque monsters were popular subjects for prints and paintings.

## Art for the Townspeople

As the merchants of the city of Edo grew wealthier and had more leisure time, a separate school of art developed for their entertainment. It was called the Ukiyo-e School of woodblock-prints and scroll paintings. Ukiyo-e means "Pictures of the Floating World." This was the world inhabited by *kabuki* actors (see page 56), and by beautiful women, where townsmen went to forget briefly the hardships of everyday life. Many artists depicted this world in woodblock-printed pinups. Later on, as more people were free to travel, landscapes and famous tourist spots were shown in prints by Hokusai (1760–1849) and Hiroshige (1797–1858), which people collected as souvenirs.

*Rich* daimyō *and their families kept writing-brushes and ink-making equipment in ornate lacquer writing-boxes. This box also has designs in gold and silver.*

## Calligraphy

By the Kamakura Period, the Japanese had developed a writing system that used several thousand Chinese ideographs, called *kanji*, each with its own meaning, besides two sets of 51 symbols, called *kana*, that each stood for a separate sound, like the alphabet. (See page 10.) Ideographs were originally based on pictures of things, and in the hands of Chinese and Japanese calligraphers, writing became an art form. A subtle change of pressure or twist of the brush could produce a variation in the tone of the ink and width of the line. A person's class, education, character, and feelings could be seen from the way he or she used the brush and black ink.

## LITERATURE

Together with calligraphy, poetry has always been a highly prized art in Japan. Under the shoguns, many warriors and prosperous townspeople wrote poetry and met at *renga*, "linked verse," parties. One person would start a poem with two lines, and the others would follow, one after the other, composing a few lines to link with what went before.

As more commoners learned to read, there was a big demand for all kinds of books. Standards of book production and printing rose rapidly. Ihara Saikaku (1642–1693) made fun of the antics of the new merchant class and their pursuit of love and money in novels such as *Five Women Who Loved Love*. Another famous comic book, by Ikku Jippensha (1766–1831), is called *Shank's Mare* and tells the adventures of two friends traveling the Tōkaidō Road on foot.

**A CLOSER LOOK**

**The poet Basho (1744–1794) created the shortest poem of all, the *haiku*. A *haiku* has three lines of five, seven, and five syllables. Each of Basho's poems contains a special word to suggest the season, and his subjects are ordinary experiences that somehow seemed important to the poet.**

| Horohoroto | Scattering |
|---|---|
| Yamabuki chiruka | The globeflowers fade |
| taki no oto | The sound of a waterfall |

***In this message, written with a brush in Basho's own hand two days before his death, he apologizes to his followers for dying before them.***

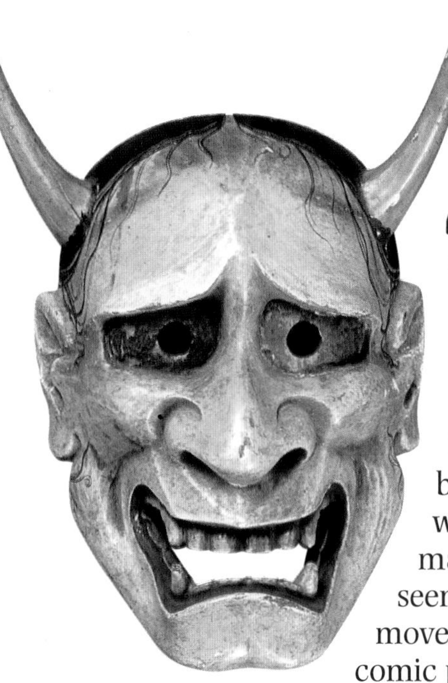

*Nō masks were carved from wood, then lacquered, and painted. This is a mask for a beautiful female character who, through jealousy, is transformed into an ugly demon.*

## *NŌ* PLAYS

*Nō* plays were originally performed in shrines as entertainment for the gods. However, during the 14th and 15th centuries, under the patronage of the Ashikaga shoguns, *Nō* became an aristocratic pastime. In a *Nō* play, the actors dressed in sumptuous costumes and mimed with slow, graceful movements. The story was narrated by a chanter with a group of flutes and small hand drums. The plots had Buddhist themes about mysterious meetings between humans and spirits from the other world. The ghost characters wore wooden masks so skillfully carved that the mask seemed to change expression according to the movements of the wearer. There were also short comic plays called *kyōgen* about clever servants who outwitted their *daimyō* masters. The *kyōgen* contrasted with the solemnity of the *Nō* plays.

## *KABUKI* AND *BUNRAKU* THEATER

Two other kinds of theater were more popular with the townspeople. These were *kabuki*, where all parts were taken by men, and *bunraku*, which was performed by puppets. The puppets were about two-thirds life-size, and seemed so real that they often had their audiences in tears. The most famous Japanese playwright, Chikamatsu (1653–1724) wrote for both *kabuki* and *bunraku*. His plays were full of cunning stage effects and impossible costume changes. They drew large audiences, including samurai.

**A CLOSER LOOK**

***Sumō*** **wrestling started in the 8th century and continued to the 16th century, as combat training for warriors. In the Edo Period, it became a public spectator sport that the shoguns tried to ban. It regained official approval only after it was turned into something like a Shintō religious ritual. After that it became popular with shoguns, samurai, and commoners. A *sumō* bout lasts only a few seconds. Each wrestler aims to floor his opponent or push him out of the ring.**

# THE MEIJI RESTORATION

The military government of Japan, the shogunate, came to an end in 1868 with an uprising led mainly by powerful samurai from the domains of Satsuma and Chōshū in western Japan. After almost 700 years, the emperor's full powers were restored. To show his authority, the new Emperor Meiji moved from Kyoto to Edo, renaming it Tokyo, which means "Eastern Capital," and took up residence in the shogun's palace. At first, the last Tokugawa shogun, Yoshinobu, was declared a rebel. Eventually he was allowed to live quietly in retirement, until his death in 1913.

The restoration of the emperor did not mean that the government returned to the old-fashioned style of the Heian period. (See page 18.) As a nation, Japan was in a weak position at the end of the 19th century, with the United States and leading European countries demanding rights and privileges. The emperor's

**A CLOSER LOOK**
**The name chosen for the new era was Meiji which means "enlightened rule." During his lifetime, the emperor was called by his own name, Mutsuhito. After his death he was renamed Meiji. This way of naming the emperor has been the custom ever since.**

*In 1906, Emperor Meiji (left) welcomed the English Prince Arthur of Connaught to Tokyo.*

supporters looked to him to take a lead in making changes that would transform Japan into a strong and wealthy world power. To gain the confidence of the people, Emperor Meiji immediately published a Charter Oath promising to "abandon evil customs of the past" and to encourage open debate.

## A time of important changes

The Meiji period was a time of rapid modernization for Japan, and many of the traditional ways of life were lost. The main aims were to build up Japan's military strength and wealth. Many Japanese people went to the United States and Europe to learn how foreigners organized their government, armed forces, industry, and education. Foreign teachers of engineering, science, and the arts were invited to Japan.

The *daimyō* and their domains were replaced by a system of governors and counties called "prefectures." Many samurai became politicians, industrialists, and teachers, and gradually the distinction between samurai and commoners disappeared. A modern government was set up with a parliament, a Prime Minister, and a Cabinet. Japan started to build factories, beginning the long process of change

### A closer look

The Japanese government thought that the treaties made in 1858 between Japan and various foreign powers (see page 31), were unfair. They allowed the foreigners to fix their own customs duties and live according to their own laws, rather than Japanese law, when they were in Japan. The treaties were due for renewal in 1872, so a group of 40 Japanese, including all the leading politicians of the day, went on a mission to the United States and Europe. They did this to show the world that Japan was willing to learn from foreign countries in order to modernize and to achieve world status.

The Iwakura Mission was led by Ambassador Iwakura Tomomi. The group spent four months in England visiting factories of all kinds in every important industrial town. They went to theaters and schools, visited the British Museum in London, and drove in carriages through the Scottish Highlands. They were received by Queen Victoria at Windsor Castle. Everywhere they went, their secretaries wrote pages of notes. Later, a report was published that can still be read today.

As a result of the Iwakura Mission, many changes were made in Japan, and the unequal treaties were finally remade to Japan's satisfaction in 1894.

from an agricultural to an industrial nation. The Bank of Japan was opened, and there were new postal, telegraph, and railroad systems. Japan's leaders realized that education was an important key to the success of all these reforms and "education for all" was introduced by law in 1872.

During the 1870s it looked as if Japanese traditions might be entirely replaced by Western innovations. Western food and dress, art and music became very popular. People began to eat beef, wear top hats, paint in oils, and play Western classical music. However, in the late 1880s, when new political ideas of equality and freedom seemed to be growing too popular, the government acted to reestablish respect for Japanese ideas. By the end of the Meiji period, Japan had established itself as a world power by winning wars against China and Russia and forming an alliance with Britain. Japan began moves to build an empire that finally led to its defeat in World War II.

After World War II, the Way of the Warrior was largely forgotten. Instead, people now feel loyalty to their workplace and work hard in order to have a high standard of living. If the leaders of 1868 were alive today, they would certainly be pleased with the degree of esteem Japan holds in the world today.

*Although Japan has seen many changes since the Meiji Restoration, tradition still plays an important part in modern Japanese life. In this picture, children, parents, and grandmother proudly wear their kimonos to celebrate a festival day.*

# Timeline

| | |
|---|---|
| **1180–85** | The Gempei Wars in which the Minamoto family finally defeat the Taira at the Battle of Dannoura |
| **1185** | Minamoto Yoritomo makes his headquarters at Kamakura in eastern Japan and starts appointing his constables and governors. |
| **1189** | Death of Yoshitsune |
| **1191** | The monk Eisai returns from China and begins to teach Zen Buddhism in Japan. |
| **1192** | Minamoto Yoritomo becomes shogun. |
| **1219** | The Hōjō family takes control of the Kamakura Shogunate. |
| **1274, 1281** | The Mongol Invasions. Both times the Mongols are driven back by fierce storms. |
| **1333** | The Hōjō and their supporters are defeated by imperial armies bringing the collapse of the Kamakura Shogunate. |
| **1336** | Ashikaga Takauji reestablishes Emperor Go-Daigo in Kyoto. |
| **1337** | Takauji puts Kōmyō on the throne (the Northern Court). Emperor Go-Daigo makes his Southern Court in Yoshino. The two courts remain until 1392. |
| **1338** | Ashikaga Takauji becomes shogun. |
| **1395** | Ashikaga Yoshimitsu abdicates and begins to build his villa with the Golden Pavilion Temple. |
| **1404** | Ashikaga Yoshimitsu renews trade with China. |
| **1467–77** | The Ōnin Wars when most of Kyoto is destroyed |
| **1449–74** | Ashikaga Yoshimasa's shogunate; central government collapses and the Period of Warring States begins. Civil war lasts until 1600. |
| **1543** | Muskets are introduced to Japan by the Portuguese. |
| **1549** | The missionary Francis Xavier arrives: the start of Japan's "Christian century" |
| **1568** | Oda Nobunaga enters Kyoto starting the reunification of Japan. |
| **1573** | Oda Nobunaga deposes Ashikaga Yoshiaki who abdicates 15 years later. |
| **1582** | Oda Nobunaga commits suicide. |
| **1582–90** | Toyotomi Hideyoshi finishes conquering all Japan. |
| **1588** | Hideyoshi's sword-hunt, land surveys, and tax reforms |
| **1592, 1597** | Hideyoshi invades Korea. |
| **c. 1600** | The Dutch arrive in Japan. |
| **1600** | Tokugawa Ieyasu wins the Battle of Sekigahara. |
| **1603** | Tokugawa Ieyasu becomes shogun. |
| **1615** | Tokugawa Ieyasu kills Hideyoshi's son and supporters at Osaka Castle. |
| **1635** | *Daimyō* are ordered to spend every other year in Edo. |
| **1639** | Iemitsu makes laws restricting foreign travel and trade. All foreigners are banished except for Chinese and Dutch, and Japanese are not allowed in or out of Japan. |
| **1774** | The *New Book of Anatomy* marks the start of serious study of Western science. |
| **1853, 1854** | Visits by the Commodore Matthew Perry and signing of the treaty opening diplomatic relations between Japan and the United States |
| **1858** | Trade treaties signed with the United States, Britain, France, the Netherlands, and Russia |
| **1866** | Alliance of leading samurai plan to abolish the shogunate. They stage an uprising. |
| **1868** | Return to power of the Emperor Meiji: "The Meiji Restoration" |

# Glossary

**abdicate** – to give up the throne.
**archaeologist** – a person who learns about the past by studying ancient sites and objects found in them.
***bunraku*** – Japanese plays performed by very large puppets.
**calligraphy** – the art of beautiful hand-writing.
***daimyō*** – Japanese warrior lords.
**domain** – land entrusted to a *daimyō* by the shogun.
**double-cropping** – a method of growing two or more crops on the same land during the same season.
**hemp** – a plant; its bark is used to make thread for weaving cloth.
**ideograph** – a picture or written symbol that stands for a thing or an idea.
***kabuki*** – Japanese plays in which all the parts are played by men.
***kamikaze*** – divine winds which the Japanese believed destroyed the Mongol fleets.
***kana*** –symbols which stand for a particular sound, used to write down Japanese.
***kanji*** – Chinese ideographs used to write Japanese.
**kiln** – an oven in which clay pots are baked hard.
**martial arts** – exercises that developed a warrior's fighting skills and strength of mind.
**Mongols** – people who lived north of China and moved from place to place feeding their herds.
**musket** – a kind of gun fired with gunpowder.
**palanquin** – a small carriage without wheels that is carried on the shoulders with long poles.
**patron** – a rich, powerful person who looks after people who have less power or wealth, such as artists and musicians.
**prehistory** – the period of time before people wrote down records of events.
**provinces** – areas of the country far from the capital.
***saké*** – a type of wine made from rice.
**samurai** – a member of the Japanese warrior class.
**sects** – groups of people who have the same religion, such as Buddhism, but practice in different ways.
***seppuku*** – ritual suicide by cutting open the stomach.
**Shintō** – the native Japanese religion.
**shogun** – a warrior ruler.
**shogunate** – the government of the shogun.
***soroban*** – an abacus; a frame with counters for working out sums.
***tatami*** – floor mats made of woven rice straw and grass.
***tokonoma*** – an alcove in a Japanese-style room where a precious object is displayed.
**vassal** – the follower of a warrior lord.
**warrior-monk** – a member of an army kept by a temple to protect its property.
**Zen** – a sect of Buddhism from China.

# Further Reading


Gaskin, Carol. *Camelot World: Secrets of the Samurai*. Avon, 1990

Hoobler, Dorothy, and Thomas Hoobler. *Japanese Portraits*, "Images Across the Ages" series. Raintree Steck-Vaughn, 1994

MacDonald, Fiona, et. al. *A Samurai Castle*, "Inside Story" series. Bedrick Books, 1995

Meyer, Carolyn. *Voice from Japan: An Outsider Looks In*. Harcourt Brace, 1992

Nardo, Don. *Traditional Japan*, "World History" series. Lucent Books, 1995

Odijk, Pamela. *The Japanese*, "The Ancient World" series. Silver Burdett Press, 1991

Sugimoto, Etsu I. *Daughter of the Samurai*. C. E. Tuttle, 1966

# INDEX